Original title:
The Beauty of a Bracelet

Copyright © 2025 Creative Arts Management OÜ
All rights reserved.

Author: Elliot Harrison
ISBN HARDBACK: 978-1-80586-144-7
ISBN PAPERBACK: 978-1-80586-616-9

## Luxurious Tales of Unity

Once I lost my favorite charm,
It rolled away, oh what a harm!
My dog gave chase, he made a fuss,
Now he wears it, what a plus!

Friends all gather, come and see,
My bracelet's gone, my dog's so free,
He struts around like he's the king,
While I just pout, this isn't spring!

**Crafting Memories in Circles**

A circle made of shiny bits,
Awkward giggles, oh, where it fits!
My friends thought it was just a tie,
Until they saw it wink and fly!

We danced a jig, we tossed and twirled,
That bracelet shone as we all hurled,
It bounced around in joyful cheer,
Now it's known as 'the circus gear'!

**Adorning Life's Journey**

With every clasp, a story told,
This trinket's worth more than gold,
It jingles loud when I run fast,
Turning heads, I'm quite a blast!

Each day it shines with memories,
Like sticky notes of sweet decrees,
But when it snags on stuff so wild,
I'm left to laugh, a carefree child!

## **A Symphony of Shimmer**

A tinkling tune from wrist so bright,
It sings a song of pure delight,
I wave and dance, it gives a cheer,
"Join the fun!" is what I hear!

But oh! What's this? A sudden cling,
The bracelet's caught on everything!
It's a band of mischief, what a show,
Its antics make me laugh, you know!

## Shimmering Reflections of Love

A loop of gleaming charms, oh what a sight,
Jingling when I dance, they bring delight.
They speak of love, wrapped tight around my wrist,
Like tiny little jewels, they'd be hard to resist.

When I trip, they jingle, a charming tune,
Bouncing off my wrist like a silly cartoon.
Each gem's a giggle, a spark of joy,
Making me laugh like a silly little boy.

## **Jewel of the Heart's Secrets**

Giggles hidden in every little gem,
Whispering stories, much like a loud mayhem.
They may be small, but oh, what a team!
A cacophony of laughter, or so it seems.

Secrets trapped in gold, shining so bright,
They twinkle and sparkle, a true delight.
Each little glimmer, a punchline so rich,
Will they ever stop? Oh, that I cannot wish!

## Artistry on a Wrist

An artist's canvas, right upon my arm,
Each bead a splash, full of whimsy and charm.
Bracelets dancing, bringing colors alive,
A clownish parade, oh how they thrive!

Doodling with gems, a playful escape,
Turning my wrist into whimsical tape.
With every move, they tickle and tease,
Like a sneaky magician, aiming to please.

**The Colors of Connection**

Colors spinning round, like a wild carnival,
Linking joy and laughter, that's the protocol.
Each hue tells a tale, bright and absurd,
A gathering of giggles, oh haven't you heard?

When friends gather 'round, they can't help but stare,
At this whimsical wonder, and laughter we share.
Each bond woven tight, with colors in sync,
A silly little circle, don't you dare blink!

## Glints of History

A charm that swings with style,
It winks at me, oh what a smile.
Each bead a tale, oh what a twist,
I wear it proudly, can't resist.

Once lost, it rolled right off my wrist,
Caught in my cat's amusing tryst.
Now it sparkles, a proud display,
Like stories living on each play.

## **Strands of Solace**

A jangle here, a tangle there,
It tickles my wrist, I cannot care.
With colors bright in fearless show,
It's like a party on the go.

When I trip and take a fall,
My bracelet's there to laugh and call.
It dances wildly, and takes the lead,
My clumsy moments, it turns to speed.

## **Echoing Grace**

Like echoes soft from times gone by,
These little gems catch every eye.
They giggle along as I skip about,
In laughter's embrace, there's no doubt.

Worn at a date that went quite wrong,
It shimmies along to my clumsy song.
But even when my charm's a fuss,
It shines through all my awkwardness.

## **Emotive Echoes**

Oh, with every jingle, there's a plot,
Where memories gather in every spot.
A bracelet's voice is soft and sly,
It tells me secrets that make me sigh.

Worn to impress my date so bright,
It flipped and flopped in sheer delight.
Now tangled up in a story's grace,
My wrist a canvas, my life a chase.

## Crafted with Care

Once a shiny trinket, so bold and bright,
Hiding all my snacks, a glorious sight.
It jingles when I dance, oh what a flair,
My wrist's a buffet, no need for a chair.

Once a fashion statement, now a snack pod,
Popping out the candies, they think it's odd.
Friends laugh at my style, but I just don't care,
Wrist full of laughter, snacks everywhere!

Each charm a giggle, each bead a smirk,
They think it's bling, but it's food in my perk.
Jokes in the jewels, it's a grand affair,
Wrist full of wonders, crafted with care.

## A Canvas of Emotions

With each shiny bead, I wear my mood,
This one screams 'happy', that one's quite rude.
Feeling a bit blue? Just watch them unfold,
My wrist tells a story, my feelings in gold.

A charm for the giggles, a bead for the sighs,
Laughter, joy, sorrow, all under the skies.
Together they mingle, a colorful show,
A canvas of feelings, vibrant and flow.

In social situations, they tell my tale,
'Don't eat the green ones, they're off the scale!'
A bracelet of winks, of chuckles, of flair,
It's the art of emotions, beyond compare!

## Graceful Encirclement

Around my wrist dances, like it's on a spree,
A chain of cute critters, just waltzing with glee.
An octopus winks, and a llama does twirl,
In moments of silence, they give a big whirl.

Every twist and turn, it's a comical race,
One floor's a giraffe, but it can't keep pace.
They jostle and tumble, a hilarious crew,
A comedy show, right here in my view!

Adorning my arm, they all have their part,
In this circus of laughter, they steal the heart.
With flair and with joy, they strut and they flare,
A graceful encirclement, full of wild air!

## Sentinels of Style

Each little trinket, a sentinel proud,
Guarding my wrist like a whimsical crowd.
They survey the scene, with glances and sass,
Like fashion police that just love to amass.

One's a tiny dog, so full of delight,
Barking at boredom, keeping life bright.
With pearls and with laughter, my arm's quite the sight,
A hilarious platoon ready for the night.

They pose for selfies, they shine in the sun,
Laughing at fashion, they know they're the fun.
Each charm holds a secret, a story to tell,
In silence they giggle, they know me so well!

**Dances of Light**

A twinkle here, a shimmer there,
Bouncing off the sunlit air.
A jingle-jangle, oh what fun,
A bling parade, we've just begun.

Oh look! It fell, oh no, oh dear!
Now it's hiding, never fear.
With every step, a clink and clash,
Making music in a flash.

Bright colors dance in happy cheer,
A rainbow wrapped, oh so near.
It catches eyes, it steals the show,
What's next? We really don't know!

A tiny charm, a dancing bee,
Buzzes around, how can it be?
This piece of bliss, a funny lot,
Reminds me of what I forgot.

**A Symphony of Charms**

A tiny turtle, a silver star,
Clinks together, dancing far.
A lion roars, a cat meows,
In jewelry's circus, take a bow!

Jingle-jangle, what a thrill,
Every charm has its own will.
It waves its arms, it struts its stuff,
Binding the silly, oh how tough!

Twirling charms in a goofy race,
Each one vying for some space.
This one's shy, that one's loud,
In this parade, we're all so proud!

A symphony of rattles and rings,
Each piece has its quirks and flings.
What a sight, what a sound,
Hilarity found all around!

## Fleeting Moments Encased

Captured laughter, a wink, a grin,
Memories locked, where to begin?
Each detail holds a tale so bright,
A snapshot wrapped in golden light.

Moments fleeting, like butterflies,
Encased in charms that mesmerize.
A hop, a skip, a joyful bounce,
Each little trinket does the flounce!

From high school dances to summer fun,
Little gems of joy, all in one.
Sparkling tales in a playful row,
A fiesta of glimmer, let's go, let's go!

Fickle friendships, laughter rings,
Nothing's serious in the bling sings.
Here we are, a silly crew,
Captured forever, me and you!

## Reflections in an Alloy

Bouncing light off polished grace,
A shining shield, a merry face.
What am I wearing? Come take a peek!
This shiny jest is not for the meek.

Oh, look! There's a face in the gold,
Is it mine or a tale retold?
Reflecting smiles, and silly cheers,
Let's wear these giggles through the years!

Twists and turns in every link,
A carnival ride, just stop and think.
Each bend whispers tales to unfold,
In this treasure, so bold, so sold!

Hilarity hides in every gleam,
What a wild and wonderful dream.
Fashion flops and friendship flair,
Forever laughing, everywhere!

## Radiance in Every Loop

In silver twirls, where laughter sways,
I catch a glimpse of sunny rays.
A twist, a turn, it dances bright,
With every jingle, pure delight.

Like tiny bells, they giggle and chime,
Reminding me of playful time.
With every clasp, a joyful cheer,
I wear my happiness quite near.

Oh, look at how they spark and shine,
Each little gem a punchline divine.
Adorning my wrist, they make me grin,
A loop of joy that spins within.

In every link, a story we find,
Slapstick moments, perfectly designed.
So here's to laughter, bright and bold,
In radiant loops, my heart's pure gold.

## Echoes of Style

With every clasp, a style parade,
On my wrist, a playful charade.
Colors collide, a wild delight,
Every angle, a fashion insight.

Bangles giggle, they dance in place,
Each reflection wears a smiling face.
Oh dear, they're quite the raucous crew,
Making me laugh in shades of blue.

Like tiny jesters, they leap and play,
Every swipe, a whimsical sway.
Echoes of laughter, rings intertwine,
Oh, what a fashion, so funky, so fine!

In this colorful mess, I have found,
A joyful echo, spinning around.
A quirky flair I proudly show,
With every twirl, my laughter flows.

## Harmony in Every Turn

In every twist, a giggle springs,
A melody of silly things.
Each link a laugh, a joking twist,
In harmony, they can't be missed.

With colors clashing, they make a scene,
A misfit gang, so wild and keen.
Dancing my way through life's parade,
In shining loops, my worries fade.

Oh, how they jingle, a comic spree,
Wobbling on my wrist with glee.
Together they sing a merry tune,
Under the sun, or 'neath the moon.

With every sway, it's clear to see,
Life's a joke, come dance with me!
In laughter's grip, we take a turn,
To a playful joy, we will return.

**Captured Moments in Metal**

Each glimmer traps a moment bright,
Like tiny snapshots, pure delight.
In this shiny album of my days,
Moments captured in playful ways.

A cheeky wobble, a restful span,
The laughter lingers, oh, what a plan!
In rings and beads, our tales unfold,
The memories wrapped in threads of gold.

Oh, silly times that make us cheer,
Reflect in metal, oh so dear.
With every sparkle, a joy-filled tale,
Each twist a dance in a wild gale.

So on my wrist, these tales will grow,
A capture of life's merry flow.
In every link, a smile so sweet,
Moments in metal, oh what a treat!

**Sparkling Memories Encased**

Dangled on my wrist with flair,
A twist of colors, joy in the air.
Every bead a tale to share,
With laughter, woes, we all prepare.

Once it slipped, oh what a scene,
Rolling fast like a racing machine.
Chasing it down was quite obscene,
Yet, here I am, a giggling queen.

All those charms, they start to fight,
Banged together, oh what a sight!
Who knew they'd hold so much delight?
Making my wrist a wild sprite!

Each gem a memory on display,
Like a circus, it steals away.
With every jingle, come what may,
My arm is where the joys all play.

## Embrace of Elegance

On my arm, a shiny parade,
Gems and colors, an art displayed.
Wobbling round like a jovial trade,
Can't stop the sparkle, I'm feeling swayed.

It tickles my skin, a dancing glee,
A twinkling talker, so bold and free.
Catching eyes with a hint of spree,
Who knew a trinket could be so cheeky?

When I wave, it gives a chime,
Blinging out in perfect rhyme.
Fancy it is, but oh, sublime,
Each glance now makes me feel prime.

Yet at times it gives a fright,
Clinging close, it might just bite!
The merry dance of this delight,
Has me laughing deep in the night.

## Circle of Unspoken Bonds

A circle clasped that tells no tales,
Whispers of friendship, tiny gales.
Each charm a giggle, craze prevails,
Oh, how it wiggles, scales and flails!

Through mishaps and bumps, we glide along,
Arm in arm, where we belong.
This clanking crew, so glitzy and strong,
We share a song, oh what a throng!

The tales we spin with each little bead,
Chasing laughter, that's our creed.
A wondrous bond, it softly leads,
In a twinkling blink, hearts proceed.

Yes, it jingles, and oh it hums,
Light as air, it dances, it drums.
With every shake, the magic comes,
Like playful puppies jumping—dumb!

**Threads of Life Intertwined**

This tangled mess upon my wrist,
A laughable sight, but hard to resist.
A tangle of joys, I can't desist,
Each twist a chuckle, joy fist!

Bouncing off walls with vibrant cheer,
It shimmers bright, drawing all near.
Cinderella's shoe—or shall I fear?
My funny bracelet brings good beer!

Every charm is a friend so dear,
Just like life, it may veer near.
With each sway, we shed a tear,
But mostly giggles, loud and clear.

Oh, entwined as life rolls around,
This silly dance, together we're bound.
With winks and laughs, we're truly crowned,
Our stories echo in joy profound.

**The Heartbeat of Metal**

In a shop, shiny treasures lie,
With charms that twinkle, oh so spry.
They jingle and jangle, dance with glee,
A band of bling, just for me.

I wear it tight, it fits just right,
But during dinner, what a sight!
A clink here, a clank there, quite the show,
My wrist, the star, steals the glow!

My friend asked, "What's that, a new pet?"
I just laughed, no needs to fret.
A creature of silver, laughs in delight,
This playful piece turns wrongs to right!

With each twist, a story unfolds,
Tales of laughter, friendships bold.
Who knew a loop could bring such cheer?
A quirky companion, forever near!

## Unbreakable Bonds

A string of laughter, clasp so tight,
Friendship wrapped in metal might.
With every charm, a giggle shared,
Stories of mishaps, no one spared.

Worn during dinners, and dancefloor spins,
This metal band knows how to win!
Not just a trinket, it's a friend,
A partnership that will not bend!

As I waved to friends, it flew,
Made a splash, right in my stew!
"Oops!" I cried, as laughter spread,
My sparkly ally, with jokes to wed.

Oh, it's a riot, what tales we'll weave!
From brake to break, truly, believe!
With bling on my wrist, we'll always smile,
An unbreakable bond, mile after mile!

## A Cascade of Colors

A rainbow of hues on my wrist does gleam,
Sprinkled with laughter, what a wild dream!
Each color a giggle, a twist of fate,
This joyful bracelet, it feels so great!

Blue for the sky, where trouble takes flight,
Green for mischief that sneaks in at night.
Yellow for sunshine that brightens the fray,
A splash of pink to chase grumpiness away!

A friend asked me, "What's with the flair?"
I shrugged and grinned, twirled it with care.
This jolly mess holds memories galore,
Like wearing a party, who could ask for more?

In parties or puddles, it's quite the sight,
With every glance, it sparks pure delight.
A cascade of colors, each hue is a gem,
This whimsical wonder, I'll cherish 'til the end!

**Precious Moments Captured**

A flash of gold wraps 'round my wrist,
Moments captured, I can't resist.
With every click, a laugh stored tight,
A gallery of giggles, pure delight!

Last summer BBQ, I danced with flair,
Got barbecue sauce stuck without a care!
But with a twist, my bracelet shone,
As friends erupted, laughter had grown!

A mishap here, a snicker there,
Each charm a memory, crafted with care.
Oh, the times I tripped, or spilled my drink,
Frozen in metal, just pause and think!

So here's to the joys that mischief can bring,
With sparkles and giggles, we dance and sing.
Precious moments, forever they'll stay,
In this jolly trinket, come join the play!

## Circles of Connection

Round and round, it fits so tight,
My wrist complains, oh what a sight!
A twist of gems, a nod to flair,
Dancing beads with quite the air.

Worn to impress or just for fun,
Watch it jingle, oh what a run!
Friends ask, 'Why do you wear that thing?'
I grin and say, 'It's my bling bling!'

Looped in laughter, a charm or two,
Their colors clash, a motley crew.
Each one tells stories, oh what a tease,
Fingers point, and nobody's at ease.

When I trip, it jingles loud,
A spectacle fits for the crowd!
But every laugh that fills the air,
Shows my bracelet's magic flair.

## **Elegance Woven in Metal**

Silver links chime with each move,
Strutting with grace, oh watch me groove!
A twinkle here, a shimmer there,
My wrist's a party, I swear, I swear!

It clinks and clatter as I sashay,
Like a marching band, join the play!
Wristwatch laughs, jelly bracelets sigh,
'How do you wear that? Why oh why?'

Tangled strands form a curious scene,
Each color pops, each angle keen.
I wave my hand, all eyes on me,
A disco ball that shimmies so free!

But when I wave, things go awry,
A hook here, a snag to defy.
Oops! There goes my breakfast, oh dear,
My fanciful bling—what a laugh, I fear!

## **Spheres of Sentiment**

Beads of wonder caught in rows,
Round and bulbous, like my toes!
Each sphere echoes laughter's song,
They dance and jiggle all day long.

Colors collide in playful chase,
A rainbow riot, oh what a place!
Friends stop to gawk, mouths open wide,
'What treasure is that on your side?'

They roll and tumble with such a flair,
Like they're competing in a fair!
Strung together, they form a team,
An oddball circus, the perfect dream.

Yet when I trip, they make a fuss,
As if to say, 'Not on this bus!'
A tumble here, and oh the cheer,
My wrist's a circus, let's make that clear!

## Artisan's Embrace

Crafted hands weave tales anew,
Wrist adornments with laughs in view.
Each twinkle shines with secret delight,
An elfin band of playful light.

Metal hugs my wrist, so tight,
Decisions made, oh what a sight!
'I choose you, oh sparkling friend,'
A love story with no end.

Or perhaps it's a prank, who can tell?
Twirling beads that ring a bell.
They jingle and jive as I strut,
'Is that a wrist or a pumpkin's gut?'

So when the world takes itself too grim,
I flash my bling; it's not so dim.
A statement bold, with humor's embrace,
In sparkling jest, I find my place.

## Illuminated in Unity

A circle of sparkles, oh what a sight,
It dances and twirls, shining so bright.
Each charm is a friend, with stories to share,
A gathering of laughter, floating in air.

With beads in a row, they clap with glee,
"We're fashionable here, just look at me!"
They jingle and jangle, with every move,
A party on my wrist, in a stylish groove.

One bead said, "Hey, I'm a lucky charm!"
While others chimed in, "We keep you from harm!"
So here we all sit, in delightful array,
Crafted by laughter, come join in the play!

Together we shine, a league of the bold,
More precious than silver, more fun than gold.
Just watch as we sparkle, no dullness in sight,
We're the life of the party, day or night!

## A Journey in Jewels

On a wrist, we ride, a comedic crew,
With each twist and turn, bringing joy anew.
We've traveled the world, through laughter and cheer,
On a quest for the snack bar, we hold so dear.

Oh, here comes the charm, a quirky old spoon,
He says, "I've seen things, dined with the moon!"
While a silver bell chuckles, "Let's ring for a treat!"
As we wobble along to find something to eat.

We trade silly tales under the sun's glow,
Like how one bead swam through mud with a crow.
Glittering together, while making a scene,
Not just a band, but a whimsical team!

So cheers to our journey, with humor entwined,
Each link tells a story, wildly designed.
We may be small treasures, but oh how we shine,
A fun-loving squad, crafted divine!

## Cherished Connections

Clink, clink, clank, a friendship parade,
Each bead with a smile, never disguised.
From pearls to straws, and a key made of cheese,
We giggle and wiggle, just doing as we please.

A heart charm declared, "I'm here to connect,"
While a tiny star winked, "What will you select?"
Oh, the laughter erupts, from dawn until dusk,
In this jolly assembly, there's never a husk.

Bonded by laughter, through thick and through thin,
We shine like the jokes that spark from within.
With every new clasp, there's more fun to reclaim,
In this circle of joy, we find life's sweet game.

So let's dance together, on wrist we unite,
With colors and laughter, we're purely a sight.
More than just baubles, we're full of delight,
United in mayhem, we glitter so bright!

## **Enigmatic Elegance**

Oh, look at me now, I'm fancy and strange,
With my charms and my jingles, I'm ready for change.
A gem that confesses, "I'm really quite sly,"
As the diamond nods, "Not as sly as a pie."

A riot of colors, each charm has a tale,
One says she once danced with a whale and a snail.
"Together we twirled under starlit beams,"
And they giggle out loud, defying our dreams.

So many connections on this wrist, I parade,
Every jingle a reminder, of mischief we made.
These treasures of laughter, a whimsical art,
A keepsake of joy, living deep in the heart.

Yet elegance thrives in our quirky display,
A mix of the charming, the weird, and the play.
We're the jewels of laughter, in unity dressed,
With a twist of the wrist, we're fashionably blessed!

## The Legacy of Love

A chain of sweet reminders, so bright,
Hugs my wrist, holds my delight.
Each charm a tale, a laugh to share,
As I dance, it jingles, fills the air.

With beads of humor, colors so loud,
It sparkles and shines, stands out in a crowd.
Gifts from friends, they laugh and tease,
'This one's for luck, and this one for cheese!'

Worn in the kitchen, while baking a pie,
It clinks with a rhythm, oh my oh my!
Every clatter tickles my funny bone,
This bracelet's a jester, never alone.

Materials are random, and styles vary wide,
But it's the memories that fill me with pride.
A legacy of laughter, always near,
On my wrist, I'd wear it, have no fear.

## Luminary Links

Oh, my wrist blinks with tiny stars,
A cosmic joke wrapped up in bars.
I swear it winked, it giggled too,
As I tripped over my own shoe!

Gold and silver, gemstones aglow,
This thing's a disco, come put on a show!
Every time I wave, it gets in the way,
Bling-blinging louder than what I'd say.

It's like a friend that loves to dance,
Twinkles and jives at every chance.
'Caution: may steal the spotlight!' it seems,
While I just trip, lost in my dreams.

As I flaunt it, the world takes a glance,
But only I know it's a tin can prance.
Yet here I am, a shining delight,
With a bracelet that slays, oh what a sight!

## Tunes of Tranquility

This bracelet hums a little tune,
When I wave hello or dance by the moon.
It sings of laughter, a melody sweet,
Who knew my wrist could tap its own beat?

With charms of joy, and bits of bling,
It jangles and jingles, what fun it brings!
'Gotta love me,' it shouts with glee,
As it twirls around, you can't disagree!

Stuck in the traffic, it plays a song,
'Buckle up, buddy, let's right this wrong!'
I join in with laughter, it's quite absurd,
A concert of bangles without a word.

So here's to my wrist, oh what a show,
It travels with me wherever I go.
Tunes of tranquility strung up with love,
A symphony crafted from treasures above.

## A Romance of Metals

Oh love, you've turned me into a multi-metal queen,
With this shiny accessory, I'm feeling quite mean!
It jabs and pokes, when I give it a twist,
'You're stuck with me, babe!' it seems to insist.

In gold and silver, a romance we share,
But at times, it snores, can be quite a bear.
A few charms dangle, in mismatched delight,
It's a chaotic dance, yet it feels so right.

Every time I glance, I break into fits,
A sparkling romance that never quite quits.
Through kitchen disasters and shopping at stores,
My metallic Valentine, I couldn't love more!

So let's clink and clatter, let's live life with cheer,
With a dance on my wrist, let's toast with a beer!
In this romance of metals, we'll sway day and night,
For with each little jingle, my heart takes flight!

**Touchstones of Togetherness**

In a box, it waits and gleams,
A jingle that fulfills our dreams.
Slipped on tight, oh what a sight,
It sparkles under morning light.

With charms that swing like happy tunes,
Each one hums like cheerful balloons.
Friends collect, we laugh and share,
These little trinkets, light as air.

A dash of gold, a pop of blue,
Frankly, it's just a fun to do.
With each little bead, a story told,
In silly whispers, and ties of old.

## Whispers of Fashion

What's that bling on your wrist?
A fashion choice no one can resist!
It jingles while you strut about,
A noisy friendship, no doubt!

In colors bright, or shades of dull,
Each clasp and charm starts to pull.
Mismatched styles that bring a smile,
They call it art, we call it style!

A treasure trove without a lock,
Fashion's silly, tick-tock-a-clock.
So join the fun, don't be late,
For bracelets are what truly make fate!

**The Craft of Companionship**

Thread by thread, we tie our fate,
In strands of laughter, never late.
A crafting hour, dear friends unite,
With tangled jokes and pure delight.

Counting beads like we count our woes,
Each charm a chuckle, as everybody knows.
A quirky piece by clumsy hands,
Together we craft our silly plans.

In this arm full of joy and cheer,
Every mismatch brings a cheer!
With each creation, our laughs expand,
We wear our hearts, a colorful band!

## **A Dance of Threads**

Threads entwined like friends in jest,
Each twist and turn, we're truly blessed.
Flickering charms like giggles sound,
In this shiny chaos, friendship's found!

A little shimmer here, a dazzle there,
Worn with love, or borrowed from air.
Swinging arms, we cut the floor,
The laughter spins, who could ask for more?

Every jangle, every bling,
A reminder of the joy we bring.
In this dance of threads so bright,
We'll laugh and twirl, until the night!

## **Luminescent Threads**

Twinkling gems on the wrist play,
Dancing in sunlight, bright and gay.
Made from wonders, all sorts and hues,
A rainbow wraps up in sparkly shoes.

That chain's a riddle, who can unlock?
Is it fashion or just silent talk?
If bracelets could chat, oh what a scene,
They'd gossip on trends and the last cuisine!

Tiny charms with stories to tell,
Every jangle gives off a spell.
If happiness had a wrist to wear,
This would be it, covered and rare.

So let's clap for the wristlets galore,
Each layer has laughter and hugs to store.
The more you stack, the fun multiplies,
With a flick of a wrist, see the joy rise!

## The Language of Adornment

Oh, what is this bling on my arm?
A sparkling circus of shininess, charm!
Are they telling tales or just playing tricks?
Whispering secrets, making me fix!

Each piece a puzzle, a riddle in gold,
What's this one saying? Oh, it's bold!
Maybe it's screaming, 'Less is a bore!'
While this little fellow begs me for more!

With beads that chatter and links that grin,
My wrist's a party where laughter's the win.
Jingly joy, a delightful parade,
Sometimes they wobble, sometimes they're swayed.

So here's to the language, vivid and strange,
These ornaments flaunt every awkward change.
On my arm, they create such a scene,
Who knew wrist bling could be so keen?

## Captured Affection

Wrist knickknacks from lovers and friends,
Each charm holds secrets that never end.
A heart, a star, and a little shoe,
What happened here? Nobody knew!

My arm's a map of who loves me most,
Each piece a feather from someone's ghost.
But wait, what's this? A glittery cat?
A friendly reminder – I can't have a brat!

With every clasp, a chuckle erupts,
Who knew my wrist was so tightly wrapped?
Each jingle is laughter, each clasp a sigh,
Like a family gathering, oh my, oh my!

So here in this chaos, joy will reside,
With bracelet charm hugs, I take in my stride.
For every jangle tells tales of delight,
Capturing moments that feel just right!

## Patterns of Reflection

Look at all these loops on my wrist,
Each one's a moment that I can't resist.
Spinning and twirling, they dance in light,
Who knew shiny bits could bring such delight?

Oh dear, what's that? A misplaced bead,
An adventure untold, a wristlet's creed.
These patterns are messy but oh so grand,
Like life's funny stories, carefully planned.

With each little twist, there's laughter to share,
As I wave my hand in the evening air.
Reflecting the quirks, the odd and the fun,
Together they sparkle – one by one!

So here's to the mismatched, bold and bright,
These splendid contraptions bring pure delight.
In patterns of chaos, I find my way,
My wrist tells the tales of this funny ballet!

## Nature's Touch in Adornments

A twinkling vine on my wrist,
Leaves whisper secrets, can't be missed.
Butterflies dance with every jingle,
Nature's charm makes my heart tingle.

Squirrels peek as I strut by,
They think it's a feast, oh my!
With nuts and bolts, they conspire,
"Is she wearing bling, or a live wire?"

Daisies tickle, laughter rings,
I wave my arm, oh how it swings!
Birds perched high look down and cheer,
"Fashion statement, loud and clear!"

In the garden, I'm the star,
Beetles boast, "Oh, look at her!"
With every chime, a giggle grows,
My wrist parade steals all the shows!

## A Kaleidoscope of Sentiments

A swirl of colors, bright and bold,
On my wrist, stories untold.
Each charm a giggle, a tiny laugh,
A rainbow of memories, what a gaffe!

Old socks and toys from long ago,
Turned into decor, what a show!
My friends call it quirky, I call it flair,
"Is that a trinket or a teddy bear?"

Dancing around, it jangles free,
"Oh dear," I shout, "don't step on me!"
Each click brings joy, it's clear as day,
Brightening dull moments as I play!

With every slip, I laugh and say,
"This mishap surely made my day!"
So here's to oddities that make us grin,
A brilliant mix of whimsy within!

## **Radiance in Circular Form**

Round and round, like my silly thoughts,
This loop of bliss has quite a lot.
It sparkles bright in the warm sunlight,
"No it's not a toy, but feels just right!"

Kids gather round to poke and plead,
"Can we borrow this dazzling bead?"
I shake my wrist, a merry chime,
"Sorry, my dear, it's my wrist's good time!"

A playful twist, I let it spin,
It whirls like chaos, letting in the win.
The sun's reflection hits each gleam,
"I'm winning this round," I laugh and beam!

In circles we dance, carefree and spry,
This circular charm makes spirits fly.
With every jingle, make it a show,
Radiance in form, where smiles overflow!

## Memories Wrapped in Metal

Once upon a time, it held my keys,
A shining sentinel, buzzing with ease.
Now it's bling, imagination's gold,
Turning my wrist into legends bold!

Did I wear it to dance, or just to eat?
"Last taco Tuesday," I gleefully repeat.
Metal catches light, a shiny surprise,
Like finding a dime in a sea of fries!

Who knew laughter could fit in a clasp?
Each click a whisper, stories grasp.
Grab it tight; memories won't bend,
"Wait, did I say we'd have to pretend?"

Nostalgia shines, I wear it with flair,
A masterpiece made with laughter and care.
So here's to the past wrapped proud on my arm,
Memories in metal, a silly charm!

## Linked Lives

Silver strands entwined with glee,
Jingles like a happy bee.
On my wrist, it takes a trip,
Looks like my wrist has joined a hip!

Each charm tells a quirky tale,
Dancing on my skin like hail.
A donut's here, and there's a cat,
Who knew my wrist could look so fat?

With every twist, another laugh,
A treasure trove, a funny craft.
I think I'll name them all tonight,
A crowd of pals, oh what a sight!

To strangers, it's just shiny gold,
But to me, it's stories bold.
I twirl and giggle, can't complain,
With my wrist, life's a fun refrain!

**The Art of Wearable Dreams**

Adorning arms with stories spun,
Like drummers drumming, it weighs a ton.
A circus of colors, wild and free,
My wrist's a carnival, can't you see?

Pandas, tacos, and a tiny shoe,
Wobbling around like they're on cue.
Every jingle's got a little joke,
Turning me into a happy bloke!

Can't wave goodbye, I'll just jingle,
A bracelet symphony, oh so tingle.
I tell my friends, don't lose your load,
Join my parade on this glittering road!

I'll strut my stuff and share a cheer,
With every charm, it's loud and clear.
In this fashion speak, I'm not alone,
My wrist's a party, and I'm the throne!

## **Emblems of Endearment**

A treasure trove on my poor arm,
Every charm has its own charm.
Tiny monsters and a fish,
Each one makes a goofy wish.

Rubber duckies bobbing with pride,
Who knew they'd choose my wrist to ride?
Hiding from thumbtacks and paperclips,
Their adventures all bring belly flips!

The weight of laughter I can wear,
Emblems of joy, beyond compare.
I wave like royalty, chime and clink,
In the land of charm, I'm the link!

So here we stand, this goofy crew,
Together we'll make dreams come true.
In this silly life, I take my stance,
With every charm, I lead the dance!

## **Poetry in Precision**

Waves of metal, a rhythmic beat,
My wrist's adorned with laughter's seat.
A pickle charm that likes to prance,
On my arm, it takes a chance.

Here's a cupcake, fluffed and round,
Rolling on laughter, what a sound!
Each little detail, quirky art,
A quirky echo of my heart.

The jingle jangle fills the air,
My laughing bracelet, beyond compare.
I flaunt it like a shiny crown,
Each charm's a giggle, come on down!

In the rhythm of my silly days,
My wrist's a poet in funny plays.
With every kitch, it tells a rhyme,
In playful fashion, I find my time!

## Stories Told in Strands

Once upon a wrist, so fine,
A twist of tales in every line.
Each charm a quirk, a laugh to share,
A little story, without a care.

One bead is green, another's blue,
They dance and giggle, oh what a view!
A jingle here, a jangle there,
A tiny circus, a crafty fair.

Each link a giggle, a silly cheer,
A memory wrapped, forever near.
With every blink, it winks and sways,
Telling tales in fun-filled ways.

So if you find it on display,
Just know it's lived to laugh and play.
A friend to dress or just to wear,
Whispering secrets, swirls in air.

## **Glimmers of Grace**

In sunlight's hug, it starts to shine,
With glimmers of grace, oh, how divine!
A sparkle here, a twinkle there,
It tickles noses, brings out the flair.

"Hey, look at me!" it seems to shout,
With giggles lurking all about.
Its shiny links chipper and bright,
Having a ball, a party tonight!

Worn on a wrist, it wants a dance,
"Come jig with me, give joy a chance!"
Each bead a joker, clever and sly,
Making it hard not to laugh or sigh.

So gather 'round, let laughter flow,
With glimmers of fun just watch it glow.
A circle of joy, it knows the score,
In every shimmer, there's always more.

## Embraced by Love

On my wrist, a hug so tight,
With laughter bursting, oh what a sight!
Each closer link a warm embrace,
A loving wink in this silly space.

With every jingle, it cracks a joke,
A twist of fate, or maybe a poke.
"Hold on, buddy!" it seems to say,
Life's a circus, let's join the fray!

Together we dance, in glee we prance,
This chain of joy, it loves to lance.
A saga told in color and glow,
Trust me, my dear, it steals the show!

So if it slips and falls a bit,
Just catch it quick, don't let it sit!
For in laughter's clutch, we laugh and shove,
This merry ride, embraced by love.

## Shimmering Links

Oh look at those links, oh what a sight,
Each one a joke, each one a light.
They shimmer and shine, full of surprise,
Giggles abound, oh how they rise!

A dainty jangle, a humorous clink,
Making mischief, what do you think?
With every shake, it cracks a grin,
Pulling friends close, let the fun begin!

They swirl and twirl, a merry bunch,
Ready to tickle, ready for lunch!
A twist of charm, a pinch of cheer,
You wear it proudly, lend it your ear.

So grab those links, let laughter engage,
With every movement, they steal the stage.
A story of joy that always sticks,
In shimmering links, life does its tricks.

## Whims of Whispers

On my wrist, it clinks and chimes,
A jolly tune of silly times.
Each charm a tale, spun with grace,
A playful dance in a silver lace.

Crafted laughter in tangled strands,
Jokes and giggles in metal bands.
Riddles of gems that twirl around,
Witty whispers that never abound.

Dancing with me through life's bright trail,
A jester's laugh in a sparkly veil.
Every bead a custodian of cheer,
Who knew wristwear could bring such jeer?

So here's to wrist toys, shiny and spry,
They bring the giggles, oh me, oh my!
Through twists and turns, they never fail,
A merry mishap, a laughter trail.

## Harmony in Handcrafted Dreams

In a wild swirl of vibrant hues,
Funky shapes, I choose to peruse.
Each knickknack laughs at the gloom,
A silly fish or a tiny broom.

Beads that chat in a playful hum,
A riot of colors, here they come!
A rainbow pillaged from a child's pack,
Crafted joy on my wrist, no lack.

Look how the daisies in metal bloom,
With witty winks, they chase the gloom.
A whimsical wonder, oh what a tease,
In a world where fun comes with ease!

So twirl away, little charms of joy,
Smiles collide, my dear wrist toy!
With laughter stitched in every seam,
Adventures unfold in a sparkling dream.

## A Bas-relief of Bonding

On my wrist, a curious crew,
Sailing forth in shades so true.
A pirate ship and a rubber duck,
They're best of friends, what's that luck?

Brass plates jingling, a band so divine,
Each charm a gossip, interlaced line.
Friends are far, but here I grin,
My band of buffoons, let's begin!

Shaped in laughter, they can't sit still,
Each twist and turn brings a thrill.
From drumming frogs to a monocle cat,
Silly companions, imagine that!

Joy in clinks, a joyful jest,
On my wrist, a laughter fest.
Each trinket holds a story worth telling,
True bonds of whimsy, always compelling!

## A Tapestry of Gleaming Stories

A shiny band dances on my wrist,
Whispering tales of laughter and jest.
Each charm a giggle, each bead a twist,
They hold my secrets, oh they're the best!

Jingle, jangle, like a merry band,
They jive with my moves, quite the sight!
I need no partner, or a helping hand,
My knickknacks and I groove through the night!

Just don't mistake them for jangly trash,
They're serious bling that can really clash!
With every swing, sentiments can lash,
A bracelet's fun, but it can also smash!

Adventures await, with a splash and a splash,
Each little gem a memory to keep.
A tapestry woven, oh what a bash,
In a world of giggles, this joy runs deep!

## **Enclosed Emotions and Wishes**

Fashioned with flair, a circle of cheer,
It sparkles and glimmers, no trace of fear.
Within every loop, jokes linger near,
Sentiments snug, watching my year!

Oh, how it giggles when I take a glance,
It knows my secrets, my wild romance.
A merry dance, not a single chance,
To fade away in its shiny stance!

Let's not forget the stories it tells,
Of days spent laughing in whimsical spells.
It jingles with joy, oh how it dwells,
In moments of madness, where everything swells!

Keeping my whims in gleeful embrace,
It tickles my senses, puts smiles in place.
With each little charm, I'm off in a race,
For life's a circus, filled with pure grace!

**Twirls of Gold and Gem**

A bracelet full of tricks, glittering fun,
Spinning tales of joy under the sun.
Twirling in circles, it's never done,
Its sparkle might make you think you've won!

Each twinkling bead a joke on its own,
Laughter encapsulated, it's cheeky and known.
Sometimes it dances, sometimes it's prone,
To trip up my wrist, it feels like a throne!

Don't underestimate the fun it can yield,
With a slap on the wrist, it won't ever yield.
It may just crack a joke, gently revealed,
In the moments when life's quirks are sealed!

A riot of colors, a gem-filled parade,
For every occasion, its magic won't fade.
It's a playful friend, in the laughter cascade,
These twirls of delight, in memories laid!

## Sentiments Worn Close

Worn close to the heart, with a whimsical flair,
Each link a chuckle, and every stone rare.
Fashioned from giggles, sewn with great care,
It dances around, giving hugs in the air!

Adorably jingly, it sings my song,
With every misstep, it still tags along.
A whimsical helper when days feel wrong,
My own little jester, where I belong!

Clanking and clattering, a cheerful parade,
It knows all my wishes, never betrayed.
In silly moments, it's clearly displayed,
That fun is the gem in this homage made!

So here's to the memories I wear with pride,
This lively companion, always by my side.
In laughter and joy, it takes me for a ride,
With sentiments close, I'll never divide!

## **Timeless Treasures**

Glimmers and sparkles, oh what a sight,
A rainbow of colors, shining so bright.
Wrapped around wrist, a delightful display,
Wobbling and jingling, come join in the play!

Each loop a story, twisted and spun,
Like a game of hopscotch, it's all in good fun.
Dangles and charms, they dance in the breeze,
Who knew such adornments could bring us such ease?

Gold and silver, with gemstones galore,
It's the perfect excuse to go out and explore.
Laughing and twirling, a whimsical day,
A treasure on wrist, come what may!

So if you're feeling down, give its charm a turn,
This silly band's glow is what we all yearn.
With every jingle, merriment sways,
Life's too short, sport jewels and play!

## Serenity in Symmetry

Such perfect patterns, in a circle they dance,
Round and round in a shiny romance.
It jests at my wrist like a playful pet,
And every glance gives me a giggly fret!

Strands entwined, like a comical twine,
Oh dear, should I wear it with glitter or shine?
Peculiar pals hang from each little loop,
They seem to laugh, forming our silly troupe!

Twinkling and tinkling, a jolly parade,
Swaying around, who needs a crusade?
Sprinkled with laughter, it's bliss in disguise,
This quirky little thing could be an ally for wise!

Lost in the rhythm, a petite escapade,
Amidst all this fun, I'll never trade.
Fingers caress, in laughter we revel,
Hold on tight, let the joy level!

## Charmed Connections

Oh look at this flair, it jingles and sings,
Filled with sweet trinkets, oh the joy it brings!
A polished enchantress, don't be shy,
Its charms wink and giggle as they pass by!

Ready for mischief, it dances on me,
With friendship and laughter, a sight to see.
Connected in giggles, we make quite a pair,
Like peanut butter and jelly, laughter fills the air!

Every charm a story, they whisper and tease,
From goofy to silly, they bring me to ease.
An ally in laughter, through thick and through thin,
Together we chortle; it's a wild win-win!

So throw on your sparkles, let comedy reign,
With joy on our sleeves, we'll never feel pain.
Wrist bling a reminder of moments that cheer,
Each jangle a laugh, now that's quite clear!

## **The Allure of Adornment**

What's that on my wrist? A quirky delight,
A shiny little band trying to take flight.
With baubles and mockery, it winks at me,
Telling wild tales in a humorous spree!

A dandy companion for tea or for cheer,
It may play a trick, it may go off the gear.
Jiggling and jostling, it steals every show,
With humor and charms, in high spirits we go!

Why just wear a bracelet? Let it perform!
It cracks funny jokes and breaks every norm.
In this shiny ensemble, life feels so grand,
We'll laugh our way through, hand in hand!

Forget all your worries, come join in the fun,
With each jingle we share, let's jump and then run!
The merrier the moments, the more we align,
So twirl in our laughter, our treasure divine!

## Echoed Grace in Every Link

A twist of fate, a shine so bright,
It dances around, a joyful sight.
On tiny wrists, it jangles with glee,
Like a puppy's bark, oh so carefree.

Each clink tells tales of laughter and fun,
A goldfish wearing shades in the sun.
With charms that wiggle, so tight and snug,
It's a party on your arm—a friendly hug!

When it clinks with a rhythm, a tune to share,
It sings of mischief, beyond compare.
In every loop, a secret shall hide,
Like a squirrel's stash, pure joy inside!

So wear it proud, let it gleam and show,
Your wrist's a stage, for the world to glow.
With every trail of laughter it leaves,
You'll find that joy, in the small and the leaves.

## Unveiling the Hidden Sparkle

Under the sun, it sparkles so bright,
Like disco balls in a wild night.
With each little flicker, it captures your eye,
A mischievous twinkle, oh me, oh my!

Like a magician's wand, it casts a grin,
Pulling smiles from places deep within.
It jingles and jangles with all its might,
Chasing away shadows, inviting the light!

It whispers soft secrets of joy to bestow,
Like a feathered friend, on a blissful go.
Oh, what a character, it leaps and it dances,
A playful spirit that joyfully prances!

So here's a toast with a wrist raised high,
To the little trinket that makes spirits fly.
Wear it with laughter, and let the world see,
The genuine sparkle that sets us all free!

## Glistening Whispers

It catches the light in the silliest ways,
Jingling and jangling through mundane days.
With every zap, it giggles and sighs,
Racing the wind, having the best of times!

A loop-de-loop around a happy dance,
It's like a grandma in her bright pants!
Each charm a smile, a memory made,
Cracking up grumps like a playful blade.

Whispers of mischief buzz through the air,
As it twirls and swirls, free as a hair.
Telling stories of fun, without needing a word,
Like a bird on a bike, oh, how absurd!

So slip it on, let the laughter begin,
With a rhythm so lively, it makes you spin.
Radiant reminders of giggles and cheer,
This bracelet of joy, it's the crown we hold dear!

## Adorned Threads of Time

Like a time-traveling train on your wrist,
It tickles your funny bone, can't resist.
Twinkling like stars in a cheeky way,
Navigating life with a playful sway!

Adorned with laughter, a dash of fun,
Each bead a sparkle, oh, what a run!
As it dances along, with a jolly fate,
It's the life of the party, never late!

With every twist, a story unfolds,
Of sock puppets and other bold tales told.
It sings of friendship, of silliness too,
A whimsical ride, just waiting for you!

So let's cherish these threads, woven in mirth,
For joy is the treasure that brings us such worth.
A wrist full of giggles, it's true, you'll agree,
This joyful adornment, is wild and free!

## Enchanting Circles of Light

In a shop of glimmering dreams,
A wrist's new friend sits on beams.
It sparkles and shines, oh what a show,
Yet who knew it sweats when I dance with a toe?

With colors that catch every eye,
It winks and it twirls like a little spy.
"Look at me!" it seems to shout,
But my skin's in revolt, oh, what a clout!

Each charm is a giggle, each link a jest,
Two hours in, my wrist wants a rest.
I trip on its beauty, make quite the fuss,
Next time I'll wear it, but just on the bus!

So here's to the circles that light up my day,
They dance and they spin in such wild display.
With laughter and joy, they jingle so bright,
But on lazy days, let's keep them in sight!

## **Timeless Treasures Bound**

Once I found a golden chain,
It whispered, 'Wear me, don't refrain!'
But every time I tried to clasp,
It mocked my fingers, what a gasp!

With charms that tell tales of old,
It promises stories, daring and bold.
Yet somehow they turn into a feud,
As it tangles up in a very rude mood!

Each gem is a puzzle, a riddle to grace,
It laughs while I search, 'Where's the clasp in this place?'
Oh, treasuring treasures can cost you your time,
But look at my wrist, it's quite truly sublime!

So here's to the gems and the laughter they bring,
Joyful ruckus, oh what a fling!
Though they conspire while I try to adorn,
They're my cherished links, forever reborn!

## Verses in Gemstone

A sapphire shines with a wink and a nod,
The brute force of my wrist feels like a prod.
The emerald's sly, with a gleam in its eye,
As I fumble and mumble, 'Why don't you just fly?'

Each bead has a tale, each link has a grin,
But when it gets tangled, let the battles begin.
I'm wrestling this wonder like it's a small snake,
And it's winning the prize, for Pete's sake!

The ruby laughs loud, says, 'Try me again!'
But each time I reach, I just feel like a hen.
They jingle and jangle, a comedic parade,
Yet somehow, their charm never seems to fade.

So here's to the verses that dance with delight,
A gem-studded journey, oh what a sight!
With humor and sparkles, they brighten my way,
In gems I confide, come what may!

## Dance of Delicate Links

In the waltz of the wrist, we twirl and we spin,
These links throw a party, oh where to begin?
I trip on each charm, like ducks on parade,
And my laughter echoes, oh what a cascade!

A jingle, a jiggle, they spring and they sway,
The clasp plays hard to get; oh what dismay!
I tug and I pull, what mischief they weave,
Yet when they are on, I can't help but believe!

Each gemstone a dancer, each link a friend,
Together they form a trend that won't end.
Though slipping and sliding gives quite the fright,
Together we sparkle, hearts feeling light.

So here's to the links that find joy in each twist,
With laughter and shine, oh they truly exist!
They dance through my days, with a comical flair,
May they always be there, a sparkly affair!

## **Glimmers of Memories**

A sparkly thing upon my wrist,
Like a little friend with a twist.
It jingles and jangles, what a sound!
A party on my arm I've found!

Each charm tells a tale, oh so bright,
Of wacky days and wild nights.
The cat tried to steal it with a pounce,
Now it clinks with a tiny bounce!

From trips to the beach to a wild dance,
Every bead holds my laughter's chance.
I might trip sometimes, oh what a sight,
But my wrist just sparkles with delight!

So let's raise a glass to this shiny craze,
Where memories twinkle in funny ways.
With every roll and every turn,
This bracelet's the star, watch it burn!

## Adorned with History

An ancient tale from days of old,
Each trinket is a story told.
From grandma's grip to uncle's prank,
Every clasp is a silly flank!

With colors bright and shapes so weird,
I think my arm has truly steered!
A dinosaur charm from ages past,
Okay, maybe I bought it fast!

The stretchy bands, a twist in time,
They wobble and jiggle, oh what a rhyme!
If only my fashion sense could learn,
But this quirkiness, I truly yearn!

So hold your wrist up high in glee,
With every laugh, don't forget me!
These baubles might be slightly absurd,
But they sing out loud—life's a happy blur!

## Chains of Silver Dreams

Oh, silver links that dance so fine,
Each one whispers, 'You're divine!'
Yet here I am with spaghetti stuck,
Sometimes I wonder if I'm out of luck.

I wear the dreams of a crowded fair,
A pretzel charm, is that really fair?
It dangles like a badge of cheer,
But mostly it's just the snack I fear.

With every twist, it pulls my hair,
This shimmery chain—what a lovely scare!
I giggle and laugh as I give it a swing,
Adventures await, oh what could that bring?

So here's to the moments, silly and bright,
Each chain holds a story, guaranteed insight!
So let's be jolly, and give it a whirl,
As my silver dreams dance and twirl!

## **Woven Whispers of Time**

Woven threads and hues so bold,
A quirky tale slowly unfolds.
With each little knot, I can't help but grin,
Who needs a crown when I have this win?

From unicorns to tiny cats,
These charms bounce like crazy bats!
Each whispering knot, it pulls me tight,
Caution: this may spark a silly fight!

I wave my wrist like it's a flag,
Declaring fun—let's be a brag!
Though tangled once with my messy hair,
Life's full of giggles, so let's not despair!

So cheer to the laughter and joy we find,
With every twist, we leave worries behind.
A woven wonder, let's dance and rhyme,
In this silly tale, we've beaten time!

## Captivating Circles

Round and round, it spins with glee,
A circle of joy, just like a bee.
I wore it once to run and play,
It bounced away, oh what a day!

The jingle-jangle brings a smile,
It dances with me for a while.
A loop-de-loop, so full of cheer,
A pet that's lost, but always near.

With charms that clink and beads that gleam,
My arm's a canvas, I'm living the dream.
If only it could walk and talk,
We'd stroll the park like a funny flock!

But just like friendships, they sometimes break,
With a heartfelt laugh, I make a remake.
So here's a toast with a silly cheer,
To my wrist companion, always near!

## **Starlit Sentiments**

What a sight, my wrist's delight,
With stars that twinkle through the night.
Each charm a wish, a story to tell,
I'd wear it to lunch, it rang the bell!

Its shiny face makes me feel grand,
A dazzling piece in a dinner band.
But when I dance, it plays a tune,
Clashing with forks, oh what a boon!

Gleaming bright, like a disco ball,
It spins and shines at every fall.
I tell it secrets, it doesn't squeak,
But when it rattles, it's my wrist's peak!

So here's my gem, a jester's crown,
From morning light till night falls down.
Though it may slip, take a quick dive,
With laughter and fun, it's how we thrive!

## Adorning the Heart

Clink-clank, my wrist parade,
With colorful beads that never fade.
They giggle and grin in every hue,
Like childhood dreams that always grew!

Worn for laughs or a silly prank,
It's like a pet but no needs to thank.
When I wave, it gives a cheer,
A jolly friend, always near!

But oh the times it tried to flee,
At the ice cream shop, it said 'wee-hee!'
Flung from my arm like a rubber band,
It flew through the air, oh what a stand!

With clasped embrace, it holds me tight,
In every moment of pure delight.
When I trip, it giggles too,
My humorous sidekick, forever true!

## A Bracelet's Tale

Once there lived a band of charms,
They dreamed of wearing all the arms.
With every jingle, a giggly cheer,
They're off to adventure, oh dear!

In bubble baths or a mud pie,
This bracelet thinks it's sly!
With fun and mischief in its rings,
It knows the joy that laughter brings.

A trinket's life, oh what a scene,
Chasing cats and dancing between.
In chocolate, it swam, what a find,
Now it's the oddest, sweetest kind!

So wear it proud, let laughter flow,
For wristy tales, we all know!
With every clasp, a tale unfurls,
Of jiving joy in this funny world!

www.ingramcontent.com/pod-product-compliance
Lightning Source LLC
Chambersburg PA
CBHW060126230426
43661CB00003B/351